Tuli Rose

The ocean's favorite color is desert

Peek Inside

Foreword: Setting Sail on Uncharted Waters

Hey there,

I'm Tuli Rose, and I've got a story for you. Not the fairy tale kind, but the real-deal kind of adventure that kicks off when you step into the wild waves of managing your own money. This isn't just a book about dollars and cents; it's about finding your path through the chaotic, exciting, sometimes overwhelming world of being a teenager — with a twist.

Think of the ocean, vast and unpredictable, a bit like life, right? Now picture the desert — quiet, steady, and surprisingly full of life under the surface. Odd comparison? Maybe. But here's the thing: even in the midst of all the noise and confusion (the ocean), there's a place of clarity and calm (the desert) that we're all trying to reach. Especially when it comes to money.

This book, "The Ocean's Favorite Color is Desert," is your map. It's about navigating those waters, from earning your first paycheck to saving for something big, spending wisely (or learning to), and everything in between. We'll dive into why sometimes the things we think will be complicated, like investing or insurance, can actually be the stepping stones to getting where we want to be.

Why should you care? Because managing money is more than just a good skill to have. It's about freedom — the freedom to make choices, to chase dreams, and to stand on your own two feet. And who doesn't want that?

So, whether you're just dipping your toes in or you're ready to dive deep, this journey's for you. No jargon, no lectures — just real talk about making and managing money.

Let's set sail, shall we? The waters might be uncharted, but who's to say we can't find our desert, our place of peace and stability, in the colors of the ocean.

Catch you in the waves,

Tuli

The Rule of Earning

Rule: Money is earned, not given.

Hey there! Let's kick things off with a basic truth: money doesn't just appear; you've got to earn it. This chapter isn't just about getting cash; it's about understanding why earning your own money is a big deal and how it can kickstart your journey to being financially savvy.

Why Earning Your Own Cash Feels Great

Earning money is more than just pocket change for the movies or saving up for that game you've been eyeing. It's about feeling proud because that money? You made it happen. It's about learning the value of a dollar, not because someone lectured you about it, but because you experienced what it takes to earn it.

Ways to Make Money as a Teen

Think jobs for teens are limited to babysitting or bagging groceries? Think again. The world's your oyster, especially with the internet. You can sell art, stream video games, tutor, or even start a mini business selling stuff you're passionate about. What are you good at? What do you love doing? There's probably a way to turn that into cash.

Taking the First Step

Don't sit around waiting for opportunities to find you. Go out there and grab them. Whether it's asking around the neighborhood if anyone needs a dog walker, selling crafts online, or offering to mow lawns, showing initiative is key. Plus, getting started is often the hardest part. Once you're rolling, things get easier.

Hard Work = Reward

Earning money isn't always easy. It might mean giving up weekends, spending evenings on projects, or juggling jobs with homework. But the satisfaction of buying something with money you earned? Unbeatable. Plus, you're learning super important skills like how to manage your time and stick with something, even when it gets tough.

Starting Small is Okay

Your first paycheck might not be huge, and that's totally fine. What matters is that you're learning — about work, about money, and about yourself. Every job, no matter how small, is a step towards bigger things. It's all part of the journey towards financial independence.

It's Your Money, Manage It Wisely

Now that you're making your own money, think about what you want to do with it. Sure, spending it on fun stuff is tempting, but saving some of it, or even investing a little, can be really smart moves. Learning to manage your money early on sets you up for a future where you're in control of your finances, not the other way around.

This chapter is your first step into the world of money management, where earning is just the beginning. By keeping things simple, relatable, and a bit fun, we're going to dive into how managing money wisely can become a part of your everyday life. Let's do this!

The Rule of Saving

Rule: Pay yourself first.

Alright, you've started earning some cash — awesome! Now, let's talk about what to do with it. Saving might not sound as thrilling as spending, but trust me, it's like a superpower waiting to be unlocked. This chapter is all about getting you into the habit of saving, not tomorrow, but right now.

Why Saving is Your Best Friend

Think of saving money as paying your future self. It might seem a bit weird to think about it like that, but it's true. That money you tuck away now? It's going to come in handy for things down the line, whether it's something big like a car or just having the cash to go out with friends next weekend.

Getting Started: Saving Doesn't Have to Hurt

You don't need to stash away huge amounts for it to count. Even a few dollars from what you earn can start your savings pile. It's all about making it a habit. Every time you get some money, put a little bit of it into savings. Think of it as your personal no-touch zone.

The Magic of Watching Your Money Grow

There's something kind of cool about watching your savings grow over time. It starts small, but as you keep adding to it, suddenly you've got a stash. And the best part? You did that. You're the one in control, making smart moves with your money.

Emergency Fund: Your Safety Net

One of the top reasons to save is to have an emergency fund. This isn't the most fun thing to think about, but it's super important. Life throws curveballs, and having money set aside means you won't be stressed about cash when unexpected things happen. It's like having a financial safety net.

How to Make Saving Easier
Let's make saving as painless as possible. You can set up a separate savings account or even use an app to track your savings goals. Some people like to set challenges for themselves, like saving a certain amount each month or cutting back on something to save more. Find what works for you and stick with it.

Celebrate Your Saving Wins
Saving money is a big deal, so don't forget to give yourself some credit. When you hit a saving goal, even a small one, celebrate it. It's a sign you're getting smarter about your finances,

and that's worth acknowledging. Plus, it keeps you motivated to save even more.

Now that you've got the earning and saving bits down, you're well on your way to becoming a money management pro. Remember, every dollar you save is like investing in your own future. So, keep at it, and watch your savings — and your financial smarts — grow.

The Rule of Spending Wisely

Rule: Needs before wants.

You've got the hang of earning and saving — nice work! Now comes the tricky part: spending. Spending money is easy, but spending it wisely? That's where the real skill comes in. This chapter isn't about cutting out all the fun stuff. It's about making smart choices so you can enjoy your money without regrets.

Figuring Out Wants vs. Needs

First up, let's break down the difference between wants and needs. Needs are the essentials: food, shelter, saving for college, or even buying books for school. Wants are all the extra goodies: the latest sneakers, video games, or that fancy coffee drink. Learning to prioritize your needs over your wants is key to smart spending.

The Thrill of a Good Deal

Spending wisely doesn't mean you can't have what you want; it just means getting more bang for your buck. Look for sales, use coupons, or buy secondhand. There's a real thrill in scoring a deal, and your bank account will thank you for it.

The Power of Waiting

Ever heard of the 24-hour rule? If you see something you really want, wait 24 hours before buying it. If you still want it after a day, and it fits into your budget, go for it. But you'd be surprised how often that urge to buy fades away. This little trick can save you from impulse buys you might regret later.

Budgeting for Fun

Yes, you can still have fun and be smart with your money. Set aside a little bit of your budget for the fun stuff, the wants. This way, you can enjoy your hard-earned cash without dipping into savings or spending money meant for important stuff.

Handling Peer Pressure

Let's be real: seeing friends buy cool stuff can make it tough to stick to your spending plan. But remember, true friends won't judge you for being smart with your money. And there's no shame in saying, "I'm saving up for something big," or "I'm watching my spending." Chances are, they might even admire your discipline.

Making Smart Spending a Habit

The more you practice spending wisely, the easier it gets. It becomes a habit, part of your everyday life. You start to see the benefits, like having money when you really need it or reaching your saving goals faster. And that feeling of financial control? It's pretty awesome.

Mastering the art of spending wisely is a game-changer. It's not just about saving money; it's about making the most of the money you have. So, take charge, make smart choices, and watch how your financial confidence grows. With every smart spending decision, you're building a stronger, more secure financial future for yourself.

Understanding the Psychology of Money

Rule: Master Your Emotions to Master Your Money.

Money isn't just a matter of numbers; it's deeply intertwined with our emotions, beliefs, and upbringing. This chapter dives into the psychology behind our financial decisions, offering insights into why we spend, save, or stress about money the way we do. Understanding this can empower you to make smarter financial choices and avoid common pitfalls.

The Emotional Weight of Money

Money can evoke a range of emotions from joy and security to fear and envy. Often, these feelings are rooted in early experiences or societal messages about wealth and success. Recognizing the emotions tied to your financial decisions is the first step toward managing your money more rationally.

Impulse Buying and Instant Gratification

Ever wondered why it's so tempting to spend money on things you don't need? It's all about seeking instant gratification — a quick hit of happiness. But this fleeting joy can undermine long-term financial goals. Learning to delay gratification can strengthen your financial future and lead to more meaningful rewards.

Social Media and Spending

Social media platforms are flooded with images of people flaunting their latest purchases, travels, and experiences, fueling a sense of lacking or desire to keep up. This phenomenon, often called "FOMO" (fear of missing out), can drive unnecessary spending. Cultivating awareness of this influence helps you resist the urge to spend based on comparison and focus on what truly matters to you.

Money Mindsets: Scarcity vs. Abundance

Your mindset about money — seeing it as either scarce or abundant — shapes your financial behavior. A scarcity mindset may lead you to hoard money or fear spending, while an abundance mindset encourages the belief that resources can be replenished and grown. Balancing these perspectives is key to healthy financial habits.

The Power of Financial Goals

Setting financial goals isn't just about planning for the future; it's a psychological tool that gives your money a purpose and can motivate you to make smarter choices. Goals help combat impulsive decisions by keeping your focus on longer-term rewards.

Building a Healthy Relationship with Money

Developing a healthy relationship with money means understanding its role in your life as a tool to achieve your dreams, not an end in itself. It involves making peace with your financial situation, learning from mistakes, and celebrating successes, no matter how small.

Strategies for a Better Money Mindset

- **Practice gratitude**: Focus on what you have, not what you lack.

- **Educate yourself**: The more you know, the more empowered you become.

- **Reflect on your spending**: Ask yourself why you want to make a purchase and if it aligns with your goals.

Understanding the psychology of money is crucial for navigating the financial world with confidence and clarity. By recognizing the emotional and psychological factors at play, you can make informed decisions that align with your values and long-term objectives, setting a strong foundation for financial independence and well-being.

Lifestyle Choices and Their Financial Impact

Rule: Align Your Lifestyle with Your Financial Goals

Your lifestyle choices — what you eat, how you stay active, where you hang out, and what hobbies you pursue — play a huge role in shaping your financial reality. This chapter dives into how everyday decisions can significantly impact your wallet, offering strategies to make choices that are both fulfilling and financially smart.

In a world where every choice has a price tag, understanding the financial implications of your lifestyle becomes crucial. Whether it's opting for a gym membership, deciding between dining out or cooking at home, or choosing how to spend your free time, every decision nudges your financial future in one direction or another.

Dining Decisions: Eating Well Without Breaking the Bank

Food is a basic necessity, but how you choose to fulfill this need can vary widely in cost. Learn to strike a balance between enjoying your meals and maintaining a budget. Cooking at home, meal planning, and smart grocery shopping can save you a bundle, while still allowing for the occasional treat of dining out with friends.

Fitness and Finances: Staying Active on a Budget

Staying fit doesn't have to mean expensive gym memberships or high-end workout gear. Explore low-cost or free options like community sports leagues, online workout videos, or simply jogging in your neighborhood.

Remember, your health is an investment, but it doesn't have to come at a premium cost.

Hobbies That Don't Break the Bank
Hobbies enrich your life but can also drain your finances if you're not careful. Focus on interests that offer growth and enjoyment without a hefty price tag. For hobbies that do require ongoing investment (like music or art), look for ways to economize, such as buying supplies in bulk, choosing quality second-hand instruments, or trading skills with friends.

Socializing Smartly
Hanging out with friends is an essential part of life, but it's easy to overspend without realizing it. Get creative with low-cost or free ways to socialize, like hosting game nights, exploring local parks, or starting a book or hobby club.

It's the company, not the expenditure, that makes these moments valuable.

Fashion and Finances

Keeping up with the latest fashion trends can be a costly endeavor, especially when brand names and fast fashion tempt you at every turn. Cultivate a timeless style that prioritizes quality and versatility over quantity. Thrifting and clothing swaps with friends are budget-friendly ways to refresh your wardrobe without contributing to the fast fashion cycle.

Traveling on a Tight Budget

Dreaming of adventure doesn't have to be just a dream, even if you're watching your finances. Planning, saving, and looking for travel deals can make trips more affordable. Consider destinations off the beaten path, travel during off-peak times, and embrace experiences like backpacking or staying in hostels to stretch your travel dollar further.

Embracing a lifestyle that reflects both your personal values and your financial goals isn't just about saving money — it's about creating a life filled with rich experiences that don't come with a side of financial stress. By making thoughtful choices about how you live day-to-day, you set the stage for a future where both your financial and personal aspirations are within reach.

The Rule of Investing

Rule: Make your money work for you.

Congrats on mastering earning, saving, and spending wisely! You're pretty much a money management ninja now. But there's another level to this game: investing. Investing might sound like something only adults do, but it's never too early to start. This chapter is about making your money grow, not just sit in a piggy bank.

What is Investing?

Investing is basically putting your money into something that has the potential to increase in value over time. It could be stocks, bonds, mutual funds, or even starting a small business. The idea is that, instead of your money chilling out, it's out there working hard and making more money for you.

Why Start Investing Young

The coolest thing about starting young? Time is on your side. Thanks to something called compound interest, even small amounts invested now can grow into a nice pile of cash down the line. It's like planting a tiny seed and watching it grow into a massive tree over the years.

Safe Ways to Start Investing

You don't need a lot of money to start investing. There are apps and online platforms designed for beginners, where you can invest with just a few dollars. Look into things like index funds or ETFs (Exchange-Traded Funds), which are great for starters because they spread out your investment over many stocks, reducing the risk.

The Importance of Research

Before you dive into investing, do your homework. Understand what you're investing in and the risks involved. It's not about making quick cash; it's about growing your money over time. There are tons of resources online that can help you learn the basics of investing.

Setting Investing Goals

Just like with saving, it helps to have goals for your investments. Maybe you're investing to buy a car in a few years, or for college expenses. Having clear goals can help you decide where to invest and how much risk you're comfortable taking on.

Patience is Key

Investing is a long game. The value of your investments will go up and down, but the important thing is to stay the course. Don't panic and sell off everything if the market dips. History shows that the market tends to go up over time, so patience really pays off.

Investing is your next big step towards financial freedom. By starting young, you're giving yourself a huge advantage. Remember, the goal isn't just to save money, but to grow it. With each smart investment decision, you're paving the way for a financially secure future. So, get curious, learn as much as you can, and take that first step into the world of investing. Your future self will thank you big time.

The Rule of Borrowing

Rule: Borrow like you're borrowing from your future self.

So, you've been rocking the money game — earning, saving, spending smart, growing your stash, and even spreading some good vibes by giving. Now, let's chat about a tricky part of the money dance: borrowing. It might seem like a quick fix when you're in a pinch or dreaming big, but it's kinda like taking a loan from your future self. And trust me, you want to stay on good terms with that guy. Here's the lowdown on borrowing without regretting.

The Deal with Borrowing

Borrowing cash means you're spending money that's not yours yet, with a pinky promise to pay it back later, usually with a little (or a lot) extra called interest. It could be a student loan for college, a credit card for emergencies, or a loan from a friend because you're in a jam. While it can be a lifesaver or help you snag opportunities, it also means you're committing future you to pay up.

Only Borrow What You Really Need
This might sound like a no-brainer, but it's super easy to slip. Borrow only what you absolutely need, not what you wish you had. Splurging on extras just because you can is a fast track to a debt headache. Every dollar you borrow is a dollar plus interest that you're gonna have to earn later.

Borrow for the Right Stuff
Taking on debt for something that'll pay off in the long run, like your education or maybe a reliable car for work, can be a smart move. But loading up your credit card for a shopping

spree? That's gonna sting later. Before you borrow, hit pause and ask yourself if this is really gonna benefit you down the road.

Credit Cards: Handle With Major Care

Credit cards can be super handy but treat them like a cactus — handle with care. The secret sauce is paying off your balance in full every month to dodge those nasty interest charges. Use them as a convenience, not as an extension of your wallet. That way, you build your credit score without building a mountain of debt.

The Shadow Side of Debt

Debt's like that friend who's fun at first but then overstays their welcome. It can mess with your credit score, making it tougher to borrow for big stuff later on (like a home). Plus, it can be a real fun-sucker, hanging over your plans and dreams. The sooner you tackle it, the sooner you're free.

If Debt's Got You Down...
If you find yourself under a pile of debt, don't freak out. Take a deep breath and make a plan to chip away at it. Focus on the high-interest stuff first, and consider chatting with a money pro if you're feeling stuck. The most important thing? Start. Every dollar you pay off is a step back towards freedom.

Borrowing ain't all bad, but it's all about doing it wisely. Think of it as a tool, not a free pass. By borrowing only what you need, for the right reasons, and with a solid plan to pay it back, you're keeping future you happy and on track. And when future you is happy, trust me, present you is gonna be pretty stoked too.

Navigating Insurance - A Teen's Intro

Rule: Protecting Your Present Protects Your Future

Insurance might seem like one of those grown-up topics that doesn't apply to you yet. But understanding the basics now can be a game-changer for your financial future. This chapter breaks down the what, why, and how of insurance, making it easy to grasp why it's a crucial part of your financial toolkit — even as a teenager.

Insurance is essentially a safety net. It's about making a small investment now to prevent a big financial hit later. Whether it's your health, your car, or your belongings, insurance can save you from the stress and cost of unexpected events.

The Basics of Insurance

At its core, insurance is a promise: you pay a small amount regularly (a premium), and in return, the insurance company agrees to cover the larger costs if certain things go wrong. It's pooling a little bit of risk with a lot of people to protect against big losses.

Types of Insurance Teens Might Encounter

- **Health Insurance**: Covers the costs of medical care. Even if you're under your parents' plan, understanding how it works is crucial.

- **Car Insurance**: A must if you're driving. It covers damage to your car, and more importantly, it protects you financially if you're involved in an accident.

- **Renters Insurance**: If you're heading off to college or moving out, renters insurance covers your belongings in your living space against theft or damage.

Why Insurance Matters

You might wonder why you should worry about insurance when you're young and healthy, or when your biggest asset is a bike or a laptop. The thing is, life's unpredictable. A broken leg from a skateboarding fail, a fender bender in the parking lot, or a stolen laptop can throw a wrench in your financial plans. Insurance helps you handle those surprises without derailing your finances.

Understanding Premiums and Deductibles

- **Premiums**: This is what you pay regularly (like monthly or annually) to keep your insurance active. Think of it as the ticket price for your safety net.

- **Deductibles**: If something goes wrong and you need to use your insurance, the deductible is the amount you pay out of pocket before your insurance covers the rest. Choosing a higher deductible can lower your premium, but you'll pay more if you need to make a claim.

Making Insurance Work for You

- **Shop Around**: Just like any purchase, compare options. Look for the best coverage at a price that fits your budget.

- **Read the Fine Print**: Understand what's covered and what's not. Surprises are great for birthdays, not insurance claims.

- **Take Advantage of Discounts:** Many companies offer discounts for good grades, taking a driving course, or bundling policies.

The Rule of Giving

Rule: Sharing isn't just caring; it's building your wealth, too.

Alright, by now you're getting pretty slick with managing your money — earning it, saving it, spending it smart, making it grow, and even borrowing wisely. But there's this cool twist in the money saga: giving some of it away. Sounds kinda backwards, right? Why give money away when you've worked so hard to keep it? Well, tossing a bit of your cash into the bigger pot can actually do wonders for your soul and, believe it or not, your wallet. Let's break down why throwing a few dollars out into the world is a power move.

Why Bother Giving?
Giving's got this boomerang effect: you toss something good out there, and it

comes back to you, but in ways you might not expect. It's about feeling connected, making a dent in the universe, or just helping someone out when they need it. And funny enough, it makes you feel pretty rich, not in your bank account, but on the inside.

Finding Your Giving Groove

There are a million ways to give back, so pick something that gets you fired up. Could be helping furry friends at the animal shelter, planting trees, or feeding folks who don't have enough to eat. When you find something that hits you right in the feels, that's your sweet spot for giving.

Every Little Bit Counts

You don't have to be rolling in dough to make a splash. Dropping a few coins into a donation jar, rounding up your change at the checkout for charity, or giving a few hours of your time can add up to a big deal. It's not about how much you give but that you're out there giving.

Balancing Act: Give Without Giving It All Away

Sure, you want to save the world, but you've also got your own goals and bills to think about. The trick is to find a happy medium. Maybe set aside a small part of your budget for giving, something that feels good but doesn't derail your other money plans.

The Feel-Good Payoff

Apart from the warm fuzzies you get from helping out, giving can actually be good for you in other ways. Feeling like you're part of something bigger can boost your mood and even your health. Plus, if you're giving to a legit charity, there might be some tax perks in it for you.

Make It a Habit

Just like saving or checking your budget, make giving part of your regular money routine. Even if it's just a little bit here and there, making it a consistent thing can turn it into a no-brainer part of how you handle your cash.

Wrapping your head around the idea of giving away your hard-earned cash might take a minute, but once you see the big picture, it's a game changer. Giving back isn't just good karma; it's a key piece of being savvy with your money. It's about using your financial power for good, and that's pretty much the coolest way to build real wealth.

The Rule of Budgeting

Rule: Give every dollar a job to do.

So, you've been earning, saving, splurging a bit (but wisely), growing your money through investments, borrowing only when you gotta, and even sharing some of your stash. Now, let's talk about getting all those dollars in line and marching to the beat of your drum. Budgeting isn't about pinching pennies till they scream; it's more like directing a movie where every dollar plays its part perfectly. Here's how to make a budget that feels more like a buddy than a buzzkill.

What's Budgeting All About?
Think of budgeting as telling your money where to go instead of wondering where it went. It's laying out all your cash — what's coming in and what's going out — and making a

plan. It's about control, not limitations. Knowing your financial ins and outs like the back of your hand means you're the boss, not your bank balance.

Your First Budget: Keep It Chill

Start with the basics: money in, money out. Write it down, type it up, or use an app — whatever works for you. Make sure to account for everything, even those once-in-a-while expenses like birthday gifts or car repairs. If your expenses are hogging more than what's coming in, it's time to trim the fat or figure out ways to beef up your income.

The 50/30/20 Easy-Peasy Plan

Here's a straightforward way to think about your money: 50% on stuff you need (like rent and food), 30% on stuff you want (like nights out and that cool new game), and 20% on saving or paying off debts. These aren't strict rules, though. Tweak the percentages to fit where you're at in life and what you're aiming for.

Budgeting Tools That Don't Suck

There's a bunch of apps and tools out there that can make budgeting almost fun. They can link up with your bank accounts, help you track your spending in real time, and even nudge you when you're spending too much on tacos. The best tool is the one you'll actually use, so shop around until you find your match.

Fine-Tuning Your Budget

Your first budget probably won't be perfect — and that's totally okay. Life's always throwing us curveballs. Check in on your budget now and then to make sure it still fits your life. Got a raise? Awesome — decide where that extra cash should go. Spending too much on eating out? Time for a tweak.

High-Five Yourself for Budget Wins
Sticking to your budget and hitting your financial goals deserves a celebration. Whether it's finally paying off a credit card or saving up enough for a road trip with friends, take a moment to pat yourself on the back. It's important to recognize how far you've come. Plus, celebrating keeps you pumped to stick with it.

Budgeting doesn't have to be a drag. It's really just about making sure your money's doing what you want it to do. With a simple plan, a tool that fits your style, and regular check-ins, you're turning your financial goals from daydreams into reality. And remember, every dollar you tell where to go is a step toward living life on your terms.

The Rule of Financial Goal Setting

Rule: Set CLEAR (Clear-cut, Limited, Evaluated, Adjustable, Rewarding) financial goals.

Alright, you're weaving through the money management maze like a pro—earning, saving, spending wisely, making smart investments, borrowing like a boss, and even sprinkling some kindness by giving. Now, it's time to zero in on what all this effort is for: setting goals. But not just any old goals. We're aiming for goals that are as crisp and clear as a high def TV. Let's break down how to craft goals that aren't just pie in the sky but real, achievable targets using the CLEAR method.

Clear-cut: Nail Down What You Want
Ditch the vague vibes and pinpoint exactly what you're gunning for.

Instead of saying, "I wanna save some cash," zero in on, "I'm saving up $300 for that epic skateboarding workshop." The sharper your target, the easier it is to hit.

Limited: Draw Your Boundaries
Setting boundaries makes your goal more tangible. Decide on the amount and the timeframe. Like, "I'll stash away $75 every month for four months to hit my skateboarding workshop fund." This framework stops your goal from feeling like a never-ending story.

Evaluated: Track How You're Doing
Keep an eye on your progress. Whether that's through an app that watches your savings grow or a good old-fashioned notebook, seeing your progress in black and white can boost your morale and keep you glued to your mission.

Adjustable: Stay Flexible

Life loves to throw surprises your way, so your goals gotta have some give. If you end up needing to redirect some funds to an unexpected expense, or if you luck into some extra cash, be ready to tweak your plan. Flexibility keeps you moving forward, even when the path changes.

Rewarding: Choose Goals That Spark Joy

Pick a goal that lights you up inside. The journey towards it should feel just as good as reaching the destination. That way, every step forward is a mini-celebration, fueling your drive to push on.

Making CLEAR Goals Real

Imagine you're aiming to snag a top-notch skateboard. With the CLEAR method, you'd set it up like this:

- **Clear-cut**: "I need $250 for that killer skateboard."

- **Limited**: "I'll save $50 from my part-time gig every month for five months."

- **Evaluated**: "I'll mark my savings progress on my calendar."

- **Adjustable**: "If I score some extra birthday money, I'll adjust my savings plan."

- **Rewarding**: "That skateboard's going to unlock new tricks and make my skate time way more fun."

Crafting goals with CLEAR intentions turns "I wish" into "I will." It's about creating a playbook for your financial dreams that's direct, manageable, and downright exciting. Let's get CLEAR

with those goals and ride them to
reality!

51

The Rule of Money and Happiness

Rule: Money's a tool, not the prize.

We've gone through a whole bunch of stuff together — how to make, save, spend, invest, borrow, give, budget, and set goals with your cash. Now, let's get real about something: how money fits into the big picture of being happy. This last chat isn't about crunching numbers or mastering money moves. It's about figuring out what money's role is in your life and how you can use it to actually be happier.

Using Money to Be Happier
Picture money as just another thing in your toolbox, like a wrench or a set of screwdrivers. It's something you use to build the life you want and fix stuff when things go sideways. The money

itself? Not the goal. It's all about what you do with it.

What Money Can't Do

Sure, having money can smooth out a lot of bumps in the road, but it's not a golden ticket to Happy Town. After you've got enough to cover the basics, piling up more cash doesn't automatically crank up your happiness. Finding joy often comes from stuff that doesn't cost a thing — like laughing with friends, making memories with your family, diving into hobbies, or growing as a person.

Finding the Sweet Spot

It's awesome to stash away cash for later and make smart moves with your money. But don't forget to have some fun now. If you've budgeted for it, it's totally fine to drop some dough on things or experiences that light you up. The trick is nailing that balance between planning for later and living it up today.

Giving = Good Vibes

We touched on giving before, right? Turns out, giving away some of your stash can actually boost your happiness more than keeping it all to yourself. Whether it's donating a few bucks or volunteering your time, helping out can give you a serious happiness high. It's a way of feeling connected and making a real difference.

Crafting a Happy Life

At the end of the day, the smartest way to spend your money is on building a life that makes you smile. What that looks like is different for everyone. Maybe for you, it's about having adventures around the globe, creating a cozy home base, or having the freedom to chase after what you're passionate about. Think about what makes you the happiest and use your money smarts to bring those dreams to life.

Being Money Mindful

Keeping an eye on how you feel about your money choices can lead to more happiness. Every now and then, take a step back and think about whether your spending, saving, and giving match up with what's important to you. Are you investing in what truly matters to you? Paying attention helps make sure your cash is working for you, not the other way around.

And that's a wrap on our journey through money management. Just remember, money is a super useful tool, but it's not the end-all-be-all. By getting smart with your finances, you're not just setting yourself up for success; you're paving the way for a life that's rich in more ways than one.

Cheers to making both your bank account and your heart full!

Conclusion: Your Financial Journey Begins Now

And just like that, we're at the end of our guide. But really, it's not the end — it's the starting line of your very own financial journey. We've walked through the basics of earning, saving, spending, investing, borrowing, giving, and setting goals. Now, it's your turn to take the wheel and steer your financial future in the direction you choose.

Start Applying What You've Learned
You've got the knowledge, so what's next? It's time to put it into action. Begin with something small, like saving a portion of your allowance or earnings, and then build from there. Remember, the best time to start was yesterday; the next best time is now. Don't wait for a "perfect" moment — start with what you have, where you are.

Patience and Persistence Are Your Best Friends

This journey you're embarking on? It's a marathon, not a sprint. You're bound to hit some bumps along the way, and that's perfectly okay. The key is to keep going. When you stumble, take it as a learning opportunity. Every setback is a chance to grow stronger and wiser. Be patient with yourself and persistent in your efforts. Success in managing money doesn't happen overnight, but with steady steps, you'll get there.

Believe in Your Ability to Master Your Finances

You have what it takes to be brilliant with money. Yes, you! It might seem daunting at first, but believe in your ability to make smart financial decisions. Confidence in money management comes with practice and experience. The more you apply the rules, the more confident you'll become. And remember, you're not alone. There are resources, tools, and people ready to support you in your journey.

The Road Ahead

As you move forward, keep revisiting the principles you've learned. Your financial situation and goals will evolve as you grow, and so should your strategies. Stay curious, stay informed, and never hesitate to adjust your plan as your life changes.

Your Journey Is Unique

Your financial path is uniquely yours. While the principles of money management are universal, how you apply them is personal. Embrace your journey, with all its ups and downs, because it's shaping you into a savvy money manager.

As we wrap up, remember this is just the beginning. Your financial journey is a canvas, and you're the artist. With each decision, you're painting your future. Start applying the rules in your life, remain patient and persistent, and have confidence in your ability to navigate the financial waters.

Here's to the start of something great — your empowered, confident journey into financial independence. Let's make it a journey to remember!

www.ingramcontent.com/pod-product-compliance
Lightning Source LLC
Chambersburg PA
CBHW070045260726
48658CB00002B/742